575

575

SNAPSHOTS IN HAIKU

俳句

R. JEFFRIES

ARCHWAY
PUBLISHING

Archway Publishing books may be ordered
through booksellers or by contacting:

Archway Publishing
1663 Liberty Drive
Bloomington, IN 47403
www.archwaypublishing.com
844-669-3957

ISBN: 978-1-6657-6215-1 (sc)
ISBN: 978-1-6657-6217-5 (hc)
ISBN: 978-1-6657-6216-8 (e)

Library of Congress Control Number: 2024912596

Print information available on the last page.

Archway Publishing rev. date: 10/28/2024

Dedicated to my wife Sarah

It's Sarah's birthday.
My life became real, alive,
when I was shown her.

WELCOME

575 is a scrapbook of 380 sights, sounds, and other glimpses into my life. I noted over a period commencing on the year's first day and concluding on its last the small beauties of each day. I've tried to find my own middle-aged voice, creakier in the joints but without a lessening of dreams. Those dreams are often weighted down by the experiences of the years prior to this collection. Any true voice is the expression of a core authenticity. Some of this expression, as with all communications, is a form of self-assessment and self-therapy.

Haiku is simplicity—brevity is the structure from which its simplicity is driven. Dating back more than 400 years in Japanese culture, the power comes from the unwritten—what is left out. What would music be like were it not for spaces between the notes? Would it just drone on with pitch, but without any expression?

Traditionally, haiku reflects sights and seasons of nature. *575* is broadened to incorporate experiences and senses. As with all haiku, these daily sessions aim at conveying a sense that is broader than those few words used.

In this set of mental pictures, some part of each day is snapped for a year. Some moments may be cute, some may be poignant, others may seem random—much like daily life folded over 365 days. These snippets come with encouragement to look for the beauty in the simplicity of small moments.

RJ

CONTENTS

CONTENTS

WINTER
-getting started-

JANUARY AND FEBRUARY

1.1.2023
-pain pills-

Wake with cloudy mind.
Sleepy, flat body and brain.
Now time to wake up.

1.2.2023
-the bathtub-

My head in water.
No sight, no smell, only sounds.
Roaring waterfalls.

1.3.2023
-my body-

Foot numb but tingling.
Neuro, spinal, chemical?
Annoying, scary.

1.4.2023
-a drop-

Drip, drip the glass fills.
Four thousand drops required.
One more, eight are lost.

1.6.2023
-louis armstrong-

Blue skies, clouds of white.
I think only love of you.
A wonderful world.

1.7.2023
-tomorrow-

Tomorrow is new.
Chance for opportunities.
Go to sleep, then wake.

1.8.2023
-waiting-

Waiting on a call.
Walked away and missed the ring.
Sadness and regret.

1.9.2023
-dogs-

Fur balls go flying.
A squirrel appears in sight.
Dogs already knew.

1.10.2023
-the body-

Dull ache in my right knee
triggers fatigue throughout all.
My body just hurts.

1.11.2023
-feelings-

Bright mem'ries of hope.
Door slams, fingers smashed, a cry;
reminder of life.

1.12.2023
-indian owl-

A hoot sends alarm.
Entry to transitions gate.
Do not be afraid.

1.13.2023
-our dreams-

Dreams are funny things;
power to drive and destroy.
Good versus bad, who wins?

1.14.2023
-root of all evil-

Money: evil's root.
Potato skin hides its rot.
Peel, smell the inside.

1.15.2023
-my grandson-

Dom, a special boy.
Soul son of Nic and Sheri.
Loves to eat ice cream.

1.16.2023
-autumn breeze-

Autumn waves disrupt.
Clear skies, light breeze, and crisp air
teasing winter's near.

1.17.2023
-sausage pizza-

A thin pizza pie.
Ocean ripped in white cheese tides.
Sausage mounds disrupt.

1.18.2023
-uncertainty-

Uncertainty is
cholesterol to the mind,
plaquing its pathway.

1.19.2023
-vanity-

Vainglory complaints
announce one's own achievements.
Own it or shut up.

1.20.2023
-parts-

I write with my left.
I use both arms to carry.
I sing with my all.

1.21.2023
-lawyer-

I say I crave peace;
my actions create chaos.
I am a lawyer.

1.22.2023
-aging-

They say it's mileage,
not age, that causes decline.
Today it is both.

1.23.2023
-the meeting-

Crowded, stuffy room.
Damp from the heat of armpits.
Hot, cold airlessness.

1.24.2023
-aging two-

Gravity makes sags.
Reminds we have not control.
Physics governs all.

1.25.2023
-aging three-

Old body aching.
Bones remember more than minds.
Scorekeepers of falls.

1.26.2023
-arrival-

Eager to soon land.
Ear pops announce arrival.
Eagerness soaring.

1.27.2023
-travel with my son-

Trip with adult son.
Joy to still be able to
share with him new things.

1.28.2023
-my son two-

But he's now a man,
able to explain to me
what I missed seeing.

1.29.2023
-memories-

Mem'ries tickle me.
I reach to wipe them away;
the scratch leaves a scar.

1.29.2023
-trips-

Trips start with a burst.
The fuel burns hot or cold but
ends with a long sigh.

1.30.202023
-canyons-

Echoes abounding,
rebounds. Or something brand-new?
Too alike to tell.

1.31.202023
-choices-

The train is coming,
rumbling rapidly toward you.
Do you run or stay?

2.1.2023
-regrets-

Sincere hope to right
wrongs since engraved on one's soul,
before time is gone.

2.2.2023
-of care-

The mystery of care
overwhelmed by acts of bad,
leaving only loss.

2.3.2023
-late-summer dreams-

Fireflies make me smile.
Dazzling in the summer's dusk.
Sad it's still winter.

2.4.2023
-chances-

Mem'ries of lost chance.
Hopeless ache from hole in soul.
Poison? Gift? Unknown.

2.5.2023
-a garden-

Small plot with good dirt.
Cas'lly pick a red pepper.
Crunchy still with soil.

2.6.2023
-surprise-

First bite of grapefruit.
Amazing smells of citrus.
Surprised the bite was sour!

2.7.2023
-birthdays-

"Birthdays don't matter,"
says ev'ry adult I know,
until you forget.

2.8.2023
-invisible-

I want to be heard.
Footprints seen, sights shared, words echoed.
Paths are to be shared.

2.9.2023
-pain-

Pains caught in silence
hurt more than when screamed; soul's seams
burst from the pressure.

2.10.2023
-weight-

Lightness is remote.
Gravity's a heavy thing.
Blocks us from rainbows.

2.11.2023
-spring-

A warm, late-winter day.
Whisper, hint of times to come.
Longer days, sunshine.

2.12.2023
-super bowl-

Super Bowl, ann'l rite.
Fun, violence, talent, sport.
Mostly chicken wings.

2.13.2023
-lessons-

Treating dogs with care
is yet another lesson
I learned late in life.

2.14.2023
-i miss rhymes-

It is not haiku.
But miss the rhymes, yes I do.
My words cheat anew.

2.15.2023
-sports-

Tranquility woke.
Sport, noise, conflict, victory.
To half of players.

2.16.2023
-tattoos-

Inking is to hide
your skin from the eye and air,
or you from yourself.

2.15.2023
-valentine's day-

A day to share hearts.
Signs of love and gratitude.
Remember why this.

2.16.2023
-therapists-

Try to find mind's key.
Roam about in the darkness.
Clues as to the "why."

2.17.2023
-dentists-

Pain followed by drills.
Numbness disturbed by vibr'tion.
Relief is not yet.

2.18.2023
-my babies-

Love of my children.
I drink after them. Soft cheeks.
Cherubs from the gods.

2.19.2023
-the vatican-

I toured a palace.
At first, my awe overwhelmed.
Then ghosts of slaves enter'd.

2.20.2023
-arrival in new land-

Landing in new place.
Industry starts right away.
Winter is coming.

2.21.2023
-prepare for winter-

One cuts, one stacks; teams
rush to prepare for winter.
Two plus two is more.

2.22.2023
-too late-

There are some who sit,
waiting for others to do.
They are asked to leave.

2.23.2023
-trying-

Reaching us the goal.
Grabbing is but a bonus.
Rememb'r the effort.

2.24.2023
-plane ride-

Sit down, buckle up.
Pressure-back into your seat.
Adventure coming.

2.25.2023
-flying-

Flying with fresh snow.
The world awash in quiet.
Awake but dream state.

2.26.2023
-worry-

I worry a lot.
Chances and losses alike
distract me from life.

2.27.2023
-beats-

My heart misses beats.
Out of step from my being.
A stumble is near.

2.28.2023
-suddenness-

Electric shock waves
to awake my troubled soul.
I return to peace.

1/28/2023
suddenness

Electric shock waves
to awake my troubled soul
I return to peace

Intermission
-daily grace-

MARCH

3.1.2023
-a prayer-

Oh dear God, thank you
for the gifts of abundance,
beyond what is just.

3.2.2023
-a prayer-

Dear God, please teach us
to be humble receiving
that over others.

3.3.2023
-a prayer-

We do not deserve
and we have not come to earn
greater than one share.

3.4.2023
-a prayer-

Teach us to help lift
our brothers without pander;
care but with respect.

3.5.2023
-a prayer-

Our grace could but be
a plight with just an adjust
to trade our places.

3.6.2023
-a prayer-

Love lifts all others.
It must be shown, not just felt,
and carried with deeds.

3.7.2023
-a prayer-

Hate ignored gives it height,
winds its arms to seize others.
Making wrong seem right.

3.8.2023
-a prayer-

God, you must show us
how to reflect such goodness
that others can know.

3.9.2023
-a prayer-

Hope in them to take,
and for themselves to then own
their own good reaches.

3.10.2023
-a prayer-

Arms are of no use
if they fail to hold, to lift,
to do what it takes.

3.11.2023
-a prayer-

Daily, give me strength
not to do but just to be,
as I learn to give.

3.12.2023
-a prayer-

Acceptance of pain.
Not concession but knowledge.
All is part of life.

3.13.2023
-a prayer-

My heart carries blood
so to extend my true reach.
Powering my quest.

3.14.2023
-a prayer-

My humility
must apply to the things that
I avoid and yet do.

3.15.2023
-a prayer-

Help me to find peace
and calm among a storm raged
within my own self.

3.16.2023
-a prayer-

Teach me to forgive
myself the things I have done
to my own children.

3.17.2023
-a prayer-

Despite my great love,
I've failed to teach what they need.
Focus but on me.

3.18.2023
-a prayer-

No pain is so great
as that which we cause our love,
breaking then two hearts.

3.19.2023
-a prayer-

Oh, Lord, how long must
I live to learn life lessons,
to leave less scarring?

3.20.2023
-a prayer-

I'm willing to leave
only a footprint or so.
But no victims, please.

3.21.2023
-a prayer-

Even better if
a room well swept could be left
for the next entrant.

3.22.2023
-a prayer-

Let me take the time
to smell the good around me
before it is lost.

3.23.2023
-a prayer-

Acclaiming the good,
keeping the bad in its place.
Which has the most weight?

3.24.2023
-a prayer-

May my wandering be
productive, removed from waste.
Focus on the just.

3.25.2023
-a prayer-

Remember my friends,
the rock on which my self rests.
Hope I give in kind.

3.26.2023
-a prayer-

And where is my faith?
Not in God but in a dream
for things better yet.

3.27.2023
-a prayer-

Hope for that coming
to answer needs, if not goals,
of my daily dreams.

3.28.2023
-a prayer-

To find a giving
openness within my heart.
Warming others' chill.

3.29.2023
-a prayer-

Avoiding my lust
for that unneeded clutter,
distracting from real.

3.30.2023
-a prayer-

And in all things, I
give thanks for that which I have
to the universe.

3.31.2023
-a prayer-

This is my prayer, Lord.
Hear my pleas and my sharp pains.
Forgive me. Amen.

SPRING
-freshening-

APRIL AND MAY

4.1.2023
-newness-

It's a new season.
Hope in the air; it's now spring.
Leap into new grass.

4.2.2023
-nature-

Thin grass blade, tall oak.
Shared life, resource competing.
Should size mean control?

4.3.2023
-crying-

Tears burst from my pores.
Despite my drive to them back,
the salts flow away.

4.4.2023
-grief-

Sobs carry old grief.
Forgotten memories of loss.
Hope for respite's hint.

4.5.2023
-*acceptance*-

A day to reflect.
Trying to accept my prayers.
To know and be true.

4.6.2023
-*loss*-

Yet time has passed by.
Chance of great wealth or fame gone.
No chance to pivot.

4.7.2023
-*peace*-

"**A**ccept it," I scream
to myself that which I know.
Knowledge burdens one.

4.8.2023
-*greed*-

Those who have, have much.
Envy, lust crawls within me.
Again, I know right.

4.9.2023
-peace-

To find peace, I strive
for my mind to be my guide
to repress my greed.

4.10.2023
-undeserved-

I once won it big.
"You deserve it," I was told.
I know that's untrue.

4.11.2023
-humility-

Gifts should make humble.
A trustee of a life treat.
Measured joy to hold.

4.12.2023
-cleaning-

A day of high winds.
Clearing dead branches from trees.
Allowing new growth.

4.13.2023
-smells-

My dog smells something.
Investigate she must do.
Pleasure it provides.

4.14.2023
-anxious-

Sitting while alone.
Dark and quiet are not calm.
Time and space may soothe.

4.15.2023
-fog-

Fog masks day from night.
All a blur weighted by damp.
Not enough to rinse.

4.16.2023
-divots-

Glasses hurt my nose.
Divots are a perch for sight.
Pain allows function.

4.17.2023
-love-

You know I love you.
A question in a statement.
Confirming the need.

4.18.2023
-frozen-

Traffic all around.
Honking crawling stress oozing.
Life frozen in place.

4.19.2023
-sarah-

It's Sarah's birthday.
My life became real, alive,
when I was shown her.

Today's a great day.
Sarah's day we celebrate.
Dawn of a new year.

4.20.2023
-springs-

Spring is here at last.
Birds chirp and squirrels appear.
Activeness returns.

4.21.2023
-skunked-

I saw a striped skunk.
Slower than its normal slow.
Even it awakes.

4.22.2023
-stress-

Bubbles in my throat.
Boiling and billowing bile.
Day of endless stress.

4.23.2023
-pain-

Regrets, ethics breached.
Life of pained memories, yet
remedies remote.

4.24.2023
-stories-

Hear old war stories.
Bouncing among my mem'ries.
Facts remain fuzzy.

4.25.2023
-echoes-

Echoes, steps trembling.
A process terrifying.
Life as a movie.

4.26.2023
-dawn-

Relief comes at dawn.
A new sky brings with it hope.
Doors allow fresh air.

4.27.2023
-dominic-

Dom is eleven.
Thoughts of him bring me great smiles.
Thoughts cause me to ache.

4.28.2023
-loss-

We yearn to mask loss.
Sadness by loss of the good.
Celebrate sadness?

4.29.2023
-silence-

We miss and we phone.
No answer deepens the miss.
Whimpers are unheard.

4.30.2023
-cold-

Cold day by surprise.
A troubled loved one calls but
cannot change either.

5.1.2023
-dogs-

Dogs: always puppies.
Heads poking from car windows.
Eyes scrunched in the wind.

5.2.2023
-pots-

Old dirt, new flowers.
Smell of peat, hint of fresh herbs.
Flower pots now filled.

5.3.2023
-words-

Power of a thanks.
Words cogent of a b'fore gift,
fuel the act's repeat.

5.4.2023
-seasons-

I love season's change.
Nature's changing of used sheets.
Crispness undenied.

5.5.2023
-ball-

Dog runs for a ball.
Only one bounce it is grabbed.
Do I catch a smile?

5.6.2023
-truth-

Truth I can't recall.
Experience or story?
Stored in my mem'ry.

5.7.2023
-lauren-

Lauren graduates.
I admire her ownership
of her own future.

5.8.2023
-a gift-

Stepson's gift of chance
to balance acceptance with
opportunity.

5.9.2023
-kids-

Are my kids for me
to be proud, or just to cheer
from by the sidelines?

5.10.2023
-depression-

Frozen, cannot move.
Sounds and sights in the background.
Echoes from outside.

5.11.2023
-depression two-

Depression, a word.
Certainly a place, a hole.
Slippery, dark, damp.

5.12.2023
-depression three-

A pill, where is it?
Remedy, rescue, some hope.
Desperation, fear.

5.13.2023
-depression four-

Paralyzed, time stopped.
Eyes wide, shifting side to side.
A clap, then release.

5.14.2023
-depression five–

Sadness it is not.
At least that would be active.
This is being stuck.

5.15.2023
-depression six–

Slight ray of sunlight.
A strand of lint floating down.
Pilotless glider.

5.16.2023
-mom-

It was Mother's Day.
With her but of narrow time.
53 is too young.

5.17.2023
-love-

My mind caught a whiff.
Not smell or sound, but a thought.
Smiling at my wife.

5.18.2023
-regrets-

Voices from the past.
Echoes of canyons distant.
Mem'ries of regret.

5.19.2023
-falsity-

Magic school buses.
Crying in their exhaust to
come worship this god.

5.20.2023
-preacher-

Once I was to preach.
Called by god to rise above.
Showing how to find.

5.21.2023
-fog-

Fog impenetrate.
It forms a shield against light.
Before feared, now sought.

5.22.2023
-negotiation-

Can't flee, must stay, fight.
Never a warrior, thus
forced to find a way.

5.23.2023
-leading-

A crown of laurel,
atop the head of its charge.
Leads us to follow.

5.24.2023
-mentor-

A friend before me
lays a mentor's path. Its track
guides without steering.

5.25.2023
-weed-

Once so derided.
Now holding promise and hope.
Relief without meds.

5.26.2023
-weed two-

Not critical but
for me, I become sluggish.
No motivation.

5.27.2023
-my dad-

Once was dad's birthday.
Strange that I never knew him.
Did I cause him death?

I confronted him.
I warned him—"Coming for you."
He chose a bullet.

Was he afraid or
just boxed in a corner?
No alternative.

Should I be ashamed?
Was I just a voice to him
echoing others?

5.28.2023
-forward-

Need to break free from
binds that constrain my advance.
Blocking my freedom.

5.29.2023
-dawn-

Light's hint of hope comes
each day with morning's first rays.
Must survive 'til dawn.

5.30.2023
-new life-

Watering new plants.
Hoping that life will soon wake.
Growth to guide others.

5.31.2023
-questioning-

Life is only hard
when you ask of what it means.
Then it laughs at you.

Intermission
-health-

JUNE

6.1.2023
-sprouts-

Life not growing dies.
As sprouts reach for air, so must
souls reach for answers.

6.2.2023
-mending-

Broken stalks can mend,
surviving another day
to tell its story.

6.3.2023
-paul died-

A friend died this week
Good man, but horrible death.
So many 'should of's.

To lose and be sad.
We mourn the loss of the good.
Measuring value.

Regretting missed words.
Thank you, dear friend, special times.
Hear me: I love you.

Regrets, lessons learned?
Assumptions misplaced, unsaid.
Words left to be said.

Goodbye, dear old friend.
Death is not an interrupt.
Extension of life.

Goodbye, my old friend.
Can't wait to see you again.
Next life it must be.

Words I wish I'd said.
Eloquence I wish I had.
Regrets I retain.

Never enough time
to say what I want to say,
Or do what I should.

6.4.2023
-a call-
Late lonely driving.
Check-in call from caring wife.
A wonderful gift.

6.5.2023
-preparation-
Weakness is required
to prepare your mind to lead.
Own your reception.

6.6.2023
-humility-

Humility's gift
to fight contentment's burden,
allowing your growth.

6.7.2023
-son's growth-

Seeing your son's growth
is too much a gift to earn.
But it is welcome.

6.8.2023
-risk-

The singer's gift isn't
his song, but the risk he took
in performing it.

6.9.2023
-starfish-

Starfish are advanced.
Their lost arms grow back, abling
them to again hug.

6.10.2023
-death-

Beat, beat, beat, beat, beat,
beat, beat, beat, beat, beat, beat, beat,
[Pause], and then it stops.

6.11.2023
-smoke-

Smoke makes my lungs ache.
Begging for a fireman's pump.
Clear out the crud.

6.12.2023
-pumping-

Ego and regrets.
The saving pump's here always.
Now go turn it on.

6.13.2023
-childhood-

When did I last run,
full speed as if I were chased?
That marked childhood's end.

When did I last jump,
Touching my knees to my chin?
Silly is sad gone.

When did I last sob,
Unashamed at how it looked?
The poison remains.

6.14.2023
-stories-

To manage a man,
you must come to his story.
He tells, you listen.

6.15.2023
-disinfectant-

Light can make healed,
disinfecting air and soil.
Blinds promote disease.

6.16.2023
-modeling-

How can I model
for my children, when I lie
and deny my truth?

6.19.2023
-lightning bugs-

Lightning bugs. Tiny
torches of portable light.
Signal summer's start.

6.20.2023
-motivation-

Minuscule drivers
of propelling energy;
strives to accomplish.

6.21.2023
-right-

Wish to do the right.
Struggling against silent weight.
Quieter, but same.

6.22.2023
-learning-

When young, our errs are
of bad acts, but as we age,
non-acts are the wrongs.

6.23.2023
-control-

Guilt to feel control
of that overwhelmed, rather
than honor of truth.

6.24.2023
-reflection-

Frazzled by mirrors
reflecting knowledge of past
events that remain.

6.25.2023
-speak-

As a young man I
felt calling from god to speak.
Words without meaning.

6.26.2023
-forgiveness-

Vision of your child
through the lens of awareness,
of her forgiveness.

6.27.2023
-gratitude-

Gratitude to wake,
knowing safety of your kids.
Able to breathe now.

6.28.2023
-neon-

Charged gas, neon lights.
Enterprise screaming "Enter!"
Repulsed or drawn to?

6.29.2023
-awe-

Humbled and awe found,
seeing that beyond control,
that impacts oneself.

6.30.2023
-release-

HELL FUCK SHIT DAMN PISS!
Words of release and passion
that can salve the hurt.

SUMMER
-heat-

JULY AND AUGUST

7.1.2023
-birthday-

Today is the day
when I say, "Go fuck yourself."
It is my birthday!

7.2.2023
-risk-

To live is to risk.
Pain- and risk-free blocks the chance
to celebrate gain.

7.3.2023
-risk two-

Denying a chance.
Life without celebration:
living without life.

7.4.2023
-patriotism-

Patriotism.
Based on spoils to the victors,
with losers prisoned.

7.5.2023
-building-

I blast from the past.
Collecting seeds dropped before.
Old youth, new planters.

7.6.2023
-evidence-

I reflect knowledge,
not of words but by my deeds.
Intent is not act.

7.7.2023
-witness-

Witness is not word.
Hearing is not head nodding.
Demonstrate action.

7.8.2023
-evidence two-

If you know someone
and yet avoid them, we know
the truth that reflects.

7.9.2923
-pathway-

Life is suffering.
All life is headed to death.
Race is to the rear.

7.10.2023
-being-

To know is to hear.
To understand is to act.
To be is to breathe.

7.11.2023
-mirror-

I saw a mirror.
Stopped by the reflection. Strange
it was not of me.

7.12.2023
-waterfalls-

I love waterfalls.
Don't know where it goes from here.
Recycles, I guess.

7.13.2023
-smiling-

I love watching dogs.
I was not aware they smiled.
Maybe I project.

7.14.2023
-selfishness-

I see your pictures.
I had forgotten your smiles.
My undesired theft.

7.15.2023
-tea-

Iced tea with lemon.
Refreshing in summer's heat.
Who's Arnold Palmer?

7.16.2023
-secrets-

Commonalities.
World of members sharing life.
But as if alone.

7.17.2023
-stigma-

Can't we list our ills
for all around us to see?
Destigmatizing.

7.18.2023
-isolation-

Do we need to own
our alone terror of pain?
Pretend it's just ours?

7.19.2023
-yard signs-

Yard signs to thus show
that our pathologies are
as common as we.

7.20.2023
-size-

Dog and cat in fight.
Size gives way to brutal scratch.
Pain? Embarrassment?

7.21.2023
-growth-

A fortunate life.
Seldom insurmountable.
Hills must still be climbed.

7.22.2023
-fatigue-

Mileage or age? Cause
of my fatigue is unknown.
Must find fuel for life!

7.23.2023
-stars-

Clouds speckled with stars.
A hint of good things to come.
Must remain hopeful.

7.24.2023
-survival-

Loss leads to fatigue.
Sadness exhausts a strong heart.
Must endure. Survive!

7.25.2023
-joy-

A child's smile. A laugh.
Happy puppies and kittens.
Brings with joy to life.

7.26.2023
-satisfaction-

Window washing and
vacuuming large open rooms.
Gives satisfaction.

7.27.2023
-heat-

Summer heat, slight breeze.
Siphons excess from your pores.
Draining to refresh.

7.28.2023
-limbs-

Summer storm. Quick, harsh.
Separates vulnerable
weak limbs from their trunks.

7.29.2023
-billiards-

Click. Click. Damn the ball.
It won't fall; is the stick bent
or can't I hit straight?

7.30.2023
-peepholes-

Dreams. Keyholes open
a slight view into the mind.
Secret to ourselves.

7.31.2023
-risk-

Love, an exercise
in risk. Our need to lay bare,
to share with someone.

8.1.2023
-decisions-

Choices can seem clear.
Self-delusions justify.
Errant decisions.

8.2.2023
-loyalty-

Loyalty. Quiet
Is, and in its strength, gives rise
to boundless power.

8.3.2023
-nic-

Today, Nic's birthday.
Celebration of new life.
Chance to gain fresh start.

8.4.2023
-grease-

Laughter. Lubricant
to slide beyond impasses
too tight to pass through.

8.5.2023
-tension-

Calibrate tension
to make it a force of strength
rather than of weight.

8.6.2023
-sources-

Blessings, not of church,
but from life's energies come.
Reminder of good.

8.7.2023
-kids-

Mem'ries of old friends.
Smiles, childish antics. Rebukes
from moms. "Get outside!"

8.8.2023
-hole-

A hole. Suspension.
Familiar. Scary yet safe.
Falseness in its name.

8.9.2023
-stuckness-

Not a condition.
A place, time, both not moving.
Waiting to be woke.

8.10.2023
-tingling-

Tingling in fingers.
Doorbell rings. Hope. Jarred senses.
Shaken from the spell.

8.11.2023
-depression-

Depression. Darkness.
Frozen time. Immobilized.
Unable to blink.

8.12.2023
-avoidance-

Faithlessness of self.
Running from one's own being.
Avoiding the truth.

8.13.2023
-preacher-

Once a boy preacher.
Called from god to spread his word.
Voicing sense of hope.

8.14.2023
-erection-

Heightened attention.
Standing erect at first call.
Warm slumber is here.

8.15.2023
-spider-

"Patience, my dearest",
says she to her next victim.
The fly is now caught.

8.16.2023
-change-

Transitions in life.
Turmoil, instability.
Lessons to learn from.

8.17.2023
-stuck-

Repeat days fog cloaked,
stifling drive to move forward.
Coma of the mind.

8.18.2023
-*speakers*-

Speakers are burdened
with telling true messages.
Hearers free to choose.

8.19.2023
-*pools*-

Swimming pools remind
us how life may once have been
before we learned clothes.

8.20.2023
-*magic*-

Dad's trick for young son:
when hot, flip over pillow.
It's suddenly cool.

8.21.2023
-*surrender*-

By slight, change the world.
Allow others grand vict'ries.
Know that you are right.

8.22.2023
-temptation-

Temptation exists
to remind us to hold close
our own core values.

8.23.2023
-notice-

A scent promises
the unknown that may appear.
A gift that may come.

8.24.2023
-lighthouse-

A lonely lighthouse.
Lonelier keeper's daughter.
Runaway at last.

8.25.2023
-reward-

"Ahhh," exclaimed one from
the first gulp of cool water
following effort.

8.26.2023
-one-

Just as we are with
cold water, we mammals share
other common needs.

8.27.2023
-community-

Dogs, rats, or humans,
our production thrives only
in community.

8.28.2023
-naive-

Optimism base.
Reason pushed aside. Naive?
Calculated risk.

8.29.2023
-mooning-

Is the moon smiling?
Do I notice a wry smirk?
Wishing or laughing?

8.30.2023
-gaijin-

Watashi wa bob-
desu. Gaijin namae.
Faking still knowing.

8.31.2023
-sins-

Sins aren't just for young.
Repeating follows beyond.
Forgive, not forget.

Intermission

-love-

SEPTEMBER

9.1.2023
-dream-

A dream. A hope. Prayer.
Finding the connection that
is the missing link.

9.2.2023
-missing you-

Only out of town
for a few days, but it seems
like eternity.

9.3.2023
-scent-

Your scent is always
with me on the pillowcase.
Allows me to breathe.

9.4.2023
-a hair-

Found your random hair
on the edge of the bathtub.
Always makes me smile.

9.5.2023
-welcoming-

Welcome home! Missing
piece restored. Able to breathe.
Can now see; can feel.

9.6.2023
-blush-

Blush at being caught.
Vulnerable. Nerves on edge.
Risk recognition.

9.7.2023
-relentless-

I hate rememb'ring
pain I've caused to those I've loved.
Too much waste of life.

9.8.2023
-ready?-

Dai suki desu.
Placeholder words used instead,
uncertainty said.

9.9.2023
-cramps-

My heart cramps of pain.
Effect of acts done others.
Too much to process.

9.10.2023
-roots-

Connections, deep roots.
Surface growth now slowed and thin.
Enough to sustain?

9.11.2023
-cost-

Life requires effort.
The gain presumed to exceed
the measure of cost.

9.12.2023
-cousins-

Familiarity
appears as though it is love.
Cousins or offspring?

9.13.2023
-substitutions-

Lovemaking is sex,
but not so in the reverse.
Hollow substitute.

9.14.2023
-lovemaking-

Lovemaking requires
drive of passion and desire.
Obligations damned.

9.15.2023
-lust-

Obligation but
without self-desire and lust,
easily is lost.

9.16.2023
-coldness-

Warm bed become cold,
left absent lovers connect.
A coldness that hurts.

9.17.2023
-receivable-

Only love given
away can then be readied,
then to be received.

9.18.2023
-illness-

Love taken isn't love.
An illness on otherwise
healthy heart tissue.

9.19.2023
-heartbeats-

Commencement of life.
On screen witness, first heartbeat.
Hard believing truth.

9.20.2023

Smell of fresh cut grass.
Life's essential smells. Wake up.
Opportunities.

9.21.2023
-fuel-

Please touch me, I beg.
I need warmth and connection
to power my drive.

9.22.2023
-mammal-

Shared common ideals.
Core mammalian need and drive.
Companionship sought.

9.23.2023
-universal-

A spark. A charge. Shock.
Propels you to seek greatness.
Universal want.

9.24.2023
-capture-

Arrival. Capture.
This might be it. Hesitate.
Reflection. More hope.

9.25.2023
-hurt-

Love doesn't require.
hurt to grow depth but instead
survives pain to love.

9.26.2023
-touch-

Power of a touch.
Uncalculated kindness
that changes the world.

9.27.2023
-passion-

Like an engine spark.
Jump-starts life into focus.
Passion awakens.

9.28.2023
-wonder-

Wonder that fades not.
Each day starts with the holy
that I am married.

9.29.2023
-my words-

Wish my words mirrored
the beauty in my intent
of love for my wife.

9.30.2023
-gratitude-

Gratitude. Values.
Quiet appreciation.
Last words each night: "Thanks."

AUTUMN
-leaving-

OCTOBER AND NOVEMBER

10.1.2023
-roars and chirps-

A lion's deep roar;
from a sparrow a chirp sounds;
more alike than not.

10.2.2023
-shadows-

Mist. Shadows. Darkness.
Echoes of soundless quiet.
Depression returns.

10.3.2023
-boulders-

Left alone to thoughts.
Shouldering boulders of time.
Quiet is not peace.

10.4.23
-vanities-

Need to find freedom
from vanities of priv'lege.
Time allows weights great.

86

10.5.2023
-tingling-

Needles from muscles
awoke from sleep. Confusion.
Same with memories.

10.6.2023
-dark hole-

Eyes closed. Still darkness
when open'd. The mind's dark hole,
where all life feels lost.

10.7.2023
-caves-

Lost in a cave. Hurt
and unable to climb out.
Trust in rescuers.

10.8.2023
-envy-

Unjust envy fails
to see the isolation
that one hides from all.

10.9.2023
-pain-

Tender joints punish.
Blocking joy from the bearer.
Preventing escape.

10.10.2023
-commons-

Yard signs listing each
of owner's pathologies.
Common privacies.

10.11.2023
-POWs-

Two men, each captured.
When freed, one thinks it's a gift;
one trapped in anger.

10.12.2023
-sinners-

First rule of bad acts:
only do one at a time.
The second tests fate.

10.13.2023
-terrorists-

Terrorists amuck.
Reminder of the first sin.
Envy corrodes life.

10.14.2023
-good?-

When intervening
in a fight, how do you know
who is the one just?

10.15.2023
-straight bones-

Bones can heal alone.
With good care they heal faster,
with straighter results.

10.17.202
-therapy-

"Just get over it!"
As with bones, souls might heal selves.
Guidance hastens cure.

89

10.18.2023
-crying-

All must learn to cry.
Tears left inside sour from heat.
Filters for the soul.

10.19.2023
-descartes-

"I think, thus I am,"
exclaimed the maniacal
child philosopher.

10.20.2023
-i think-

To all the man adds.
"Da to omoimasu."
Degreed irony.

10.21.2023
-my mom-

It's my mom's birthday.
I claim we were never close.
Yet I hear her voice.

[echo]
It's my mom's birthday.

10.22.2023
-inflection-

Liked to hang with girls.
Learned a feminine word style.
Don't try to judge me.

10.23.2023
-perspective-

Only the taller
can assess height of one less.
Perspective required.

10.24.2023
-bitten-

The dog bite looks small,
boldly claims one not bitten.
To me, hurts like hell.

10.25.2023
-autumn-

Changing leaves welcome
fresh, crisp air to purge the weight
of summer's decay.

10.26.2023
-performance-

Forgiveness appealed
surpasses in might that of
perfect performance.

10.27.2023
-intent-

Intent realized,
when paired with effort, broadcasts
true great performance.

10.28.2023
-peace-

Peace comes from knowing
that which is not clearly said
but heard nonetheless.

10.29.2023
-unjust-

Power absent just—
abuse beyond words. Leaving
trail of men swallowed.

10.30.2023
-delays-

An airplane delay,
daring complaint of events
which we can't control.

10.31.2023
-service-

Customer service
should not be so hard. Thank you;
Please; I am sorry.

11.1.23
-decisions-

Hard can be simple.
Choices seeming unclear must
be brought to their core.

11.2.2023
-guests-

Friends from out of town.
Long overdue visit. I
forget it's so nice.

11.3.2023
-crickets-

Late summer crickets.
Start early. Air filled with sounds,
smells of transition.

11.4.2023
-best job-

The best job in life
is picking the March Madness
sixty-four teams? No.

11.5.2023
-next best-

The best job in life—
choosing when widths of ties change
style—fat or thin? No.

11.6.2023
-ultimate-

The best job in life
is being the ranker of
sins from bad to worse.

Mine are never worse.

11.7.2023
-cherish-

Cherish is to know
that to have none is painful.
Like losing a limb.

11.8.2023
-aging-

Age is a burglar.
Sneaks in to steal your most core
and unique assets.

11.9.2023
-sprains-

Why does a sprain hurt
more than a break? Healing slows,
dragging entirety.

11.10.2023
-temperature-

Looking out windows.
Empathy in trying to
feel temperature.

11.11.2023
-water-

Ocean spray on face.
Hot shower clears pers'prous beads.
Gulp of cold water.

11.12.2023
-panic-

Sudden. Surprising.
Overwhelming fear. Panic.
Will it ever stop?

11.13.2023
-swans-

Image: floating grace.
Serene yet watchful. Keeper
of castle secrets.

11.14.2023
-hitchhiking-

Bent. Marker in hand.
Drawing letters for free ride
to destination.

11.15.2023
-fujiyama-

Snow peaks in distance.
Rising from surrounding flat.
Quiet, crackling snow.

11.16.2023
-fear-

Pain: Fear in waiting?
Creeping expectation of
the yet unforeseen.

11.17.2023
-poetry-

What's a good poem?
Efforts in words, or patience
allowed editing?

11.18.2023
-airplanes-

Time now to exit.
All stand and compare heights, looks.
Gathering luggage.

11.19.2023
-etching-

Fatigue. Ache to core.
Cost paid not with time, but with
etching on your soul.

11.20.2023
-turns-

Driving. Aware you
don't care if you fail to make
the next turn. Fatigue.

11.21.2023
-fear-

Heart beating. Loudly.
Can others hear? Can they feel
the fear that I know?

11.22.2023
-failure-

Public failure. Fear
of being found to be fake.
Lifetime insecure.

11.23.2023
-thanksgiving-

Pass the turkey, please.
"What do you mean by that?" snarked
child home for visit.

11.24.2023
-traditions-

The holiday is
special not because of the
pilgrims, but despite.

11.25.2023
-prejudice-

Xenophobia—
one word takes all syllables
as air in the world.

11.26.2023
-cringeworthy-

Body purging woes.
Diarrhea of the soul.
Cringing for words said.

11.27.2023
-memories-

Which dream is better?
Of the past or the future?
Are they not the same?

11.28.2023
-memories two-

Do I remember
events, or only stories
told me by others?

11.29.2023
-real-

Facts or emotion
which builds upon the realness
of that I live with.

11.30.2023
-lessons two-

Torture is the taunt
that we must learn that needed
within one lifetime.

Intermission
-reflection-

DECEMBER

12.1.2023
-trust-

Trust can suddenly
be stolen by a single
errant, thoughtless act.

12.2.2023
-sleep-

Slept through tornados,
hurricanes, earthquakes, and floods.
Then I turned forty.

12.3.2023
-limits-

Age ticks not of time,
but of inability
to do as you've done.

12.4.2023
-history-

History does not warn
of future. It confirms what
no longer matters.

12.5.2023
-patience-

Patience comes with age.
Not time, not wisdom. Fatigue
conspires with events.

12.6.2023
-dreams-

Dreams aren't always of
the future. They can be of
mem'ries of the past.

12.7.2023
-wars-

Old men and children
left to fight the final wars.
Remnants of what was.

12.8.2023
-guns-

"Guns don't kill people,"
said the village idiot.
People kill people?

12.9.2023
-history-

One man's history
may be all that is written,
but is it the truth?

12.10.2023
-finesse-

Little strength is requir'd
to jerk a heavy object.
Gentle requires much.

12.11.2023
-heroism-

Heroes. Doing that
for others' benefit when
there's risk to one's self.

12.12.2023
-quietly-

Greatest heroes are
those who do so quietly,
only known to them.

12.13.2023
-addition-

Magic occurs when
two plus two is five or more.
Why we are social.

12.14.2023
-peace-

To know peace is to
know of one's place in the world,
free of delusions.

12.15.2023
-hope-

To have hope means one
possesses the drive to live
yet another day.

12.16.2023
-joy-

To have joy is to
give up assessing one's own
place against others.

12.17.2023
-words-

Don't say the words. Once
spoken, history is then set,
not to be undone.

12.18.2023
-balance-

Being in balance.
Achievement? Resignation?
Changes by the day.

12.19.2023
-body language-

Dogs pant; people squirm.
Acts that speak in ways words can't.
List'ning silently.

12.20.2023
-understanding-

Hearing absent words.
Doing while still. And knowing
with no description.

12.21.2023
-life-

Breathing. Taking in
life, its scents, its sounds, its sights—
the magic of life.

12.22.2023
-life two-

Cocktail mixture of
life's experiences. A
drink for the ages.

12.23.2023
-life three-

Hope my children find
mastery over life in
ways obscure to me.

12.24.2023
-misdirection-

How do you reach an
age only to find your map
misdirected you?

12.29.2023
-newness-

Sunset. A respite.
Moment of peace for healing.
Sleep and new start, soon.

12.30.2023
-repeat-

Dawn. Both fresh and worn.
New and repeat, rotating.
Now echoes off each.

12.31.2023
-ending-

Same day each year to
reflect on loss, gains, old, new.
Watching lint floating.

R. Jeffries is a middle-aged man living in 'fly-over' country in the middle of America. He continues to work through the challenges and complexities of life while trying to carve out time and space to notice glimpses into the beauty of each day.